Savarkar A Hard Hidden Hero

Savarkar A Hard Hidden Hero

Table of Contents

Savarkar: A Hard Hidden Hero

Ram Nivas Kumar
MA (English), MJMC, MLISc., Dip-In-OA

Savarkar: A Hard Hidden Hero

Edition
2024
© Ram Nivas Kumar
First published 2022

Preface

It has been a red-hot issue of discussion amongst the countrymen as well as the political giants whether Savarkar was really a true nationalist and a freedom fighter, or he was a big black traitor. Some say—he was a nationalist; some call him a rationalist. Most of the people consider him a true hero, while a few of them take him as a traitor. People at large are widely confused in the matter of grasping his real picture and understanding his exact role in India's freedom movement. There is a mess-up of all and everything. Even the learned persons are bewitched.

Meanwhile, in a twitter salutation to Savarkar, our Hon'ble Prime Minister saluted him for his emphasis on social reforms and remembered his writing & poetry that ignites the sparks of patriotism amongst the people. He further added that Savarkar will always be remembered for his patriotic spirit. He said—"He was also a prolific writer and social reformer. We remember him for his bravery, motivating several others to join the freedom struggle, and emphasis on social reforms." This left the country in high hustle.

In such a commotion prevailing in and around our country, I pondered day and night for a long over the true picture and right colour of this hard-hit human. Later, It occurred to me high that I must write a book on Savarkar elaborating all important nuggets related to him. Hence, I decided to go deep into a research on this issue. And as such, I went through a number of books on Savarkar and found him to be a true nationalist, working especially for the cause of the mass society in India. Hence, presentation of this book to the high hearts of the Indian nationalists.

Contents of this book have been gratefully extracted from several books on and by Savarkar. Some items available on highly reputed and authentic educational websites have been verified and added. Some more contents in Hindi have been supplied with by my literary friends such as ShriHari Narayan Gupta, ShriUday Narayan Singh andShriKamlesh Mishra which have been transliterated and included in the book.

No book is always fully complete. I do not claim this one to be so. While publishing, I tried hard to make this book errorproof. However, to err is human. Errors, crept in inadvertently, if any, may please be communicated to enable me rectify them at the earliest.

Hope, this book will satiate the hunger of the masses willing to know the real facts and figures on Savarkar. Comments and suggestions are most welcome.

—Ram Nivas Kumar

Table of Contents

1

Brief History of Savarkar

Savarkar was born on 28 May, 1883 in the village of Bhagur, near the city of Nashik, Maharashtra. His full name was Vinayak Damodar Savarkar. He was a revolutionary freedom fighter, high-ranked politician, learned lawyer and a vibrant social reformer. His father's name was Damodparant Savarkar and mother Radhabai Savarkar. He was strongly influenced by his elder brother (Babararo). He belonged to a Chitpavan Brahmin Hindu family.

He had two brothers, Ganesh and Narayan, and a sister, Mainabai. He was educated at the local Shivaji High School before he enrolled in the Ferguson College, Poona, in 1902. Here he involved himself in Indian nationalist politics before being expelled from college for his activities.

He created the ideology of "Hindutva" (Hinduness) in 1923. He used the term 'Hindutva' to describe 'Hinduness' or the 'quality of being a Hindu'. He regarded Hinduism as an ethnic, cultural and political identity. He died on 26 February, 1966 at the age of 83 in Bombay, Maharastra,

Hindus, according to Savarkar, are those who consider India to be the land in which their ancestors lived, as well as the land in which their religion originated. He advocated strongly the creation of a Hindu state.

Savarkar was a great revolutionary freedom fighter, visionary thinker, prolific writer & outstanding orator. He was also a social reformer who strove to eradicate social evils like untouchability and the caste system from society.

Mahatma Gandhi once said about Savarkar: "He is a patriot. He is frankly a revolutionary. The evil, in its hideous form of the present system of Government, he saw much earlier than I did. He is in the Andamans for having loved India too well. Under a just Government, he would be occupying a high office."

Savarkar spent nearly one third of his life in some form of confinement—jails and restricted movement—before he died, aged 83, in 1966. "He was a bundle of contradictions and a historian's enigma," writes Dr Sampath.

2

Savarkar's Views on Cow

Savarkar is known today as the author of the work "Hindutva", the seminal text for Hindu nationalists. But what he is little known for is his staunch opposition to cow worship. The cow was, for him, a highly useful animal, but its worship, he argued, made no sense because humans needed to worship something or someone who was super-human or endowed with super-human qualities, not an "out-and-out" animal inferior to humankind.

He called for the abandonment of the "naive practice" because it was "buddhihatya" or "murder of the intellect". He was not against the nurturing of cows and in fact assiduously promoted the principle of nurture as a "national duty", so long as it was predicated on broader economic and scientific principles – as it was, he stressed, in America – that helped maximize bovine usefulness.

But his standout line on the subject was: "We need cow care, not worship". He particularly abhorred the then widely prevalent habit of consuming cow urine and, in some cases, even cow dung. He believed that this practice might have actually started out in ancient India as a form of punishment so that a person could "expiate his sins."

And to those orthodox Hindus who thought his views were blasphemous, Savarkar had only one sardonic thing to say: Your blasphemy's far, far bigger, just see how you've crammed thirty three crore deities into a cow's belly.

Forget India's Left, even its centrists had been loath to touch Savarkar with a barge pole for decades. Some of them have now discovered him all of a sudden and taken to quoting his aforementioned views. A national leader said at a recent function that Savarkar regarded the cow as a useful animal, nothing more.

That, of course, is correct, and his views are particularly instructive in the wake of what's happening all around us. But the avowed "secularists" and self-confirmed "liberals" among us may perhaps want to read his writings on the subject a little more closely before they throw the book at the Hindutva-wadis, because of Savarkar's stand on the cow.

Savarkar did not believe that India had been subjugated only during the British Raj. Unlike Nehru who put forward the idea of a 'composite culture', he saw the many hundred years of Islamic rule as an era of shackles, submission, suppression and slavery. And one of his major issues with cow worship, apart from its deadening of the mind as he saw it, was that it had "ensured" many a Hindu defeat in the past. To use a bad pun which he didn't, it had engendered cowardice.

He alleged that Muslim armies had often used cows as a shield during key battles against the Hindus. When Hindu forces marched on Multan, he said, the Muslims had threatened to destroy the famous Sun temple there as a warning, and when MalharraoHolkar, a Maratha chieftain, had sought to "liberate" Kashi, the Muslims had again threatened to defile all things holy to the Hindus, Savarkar said and castigated India's majority community for backtracking at such moments for fear of being responsible for the razing of temples, the humiliation of Brahmins and cow slaughter.

He said: If the Hindu Rashtra, as he saw it, was ever to be hemmed in by non-Hindu forces, and there was no way out of the siege to get food, cow slaughter had to be exercised as an option. The Hindus had done considerable damage to their cause, he said, by saving a few cows used as shields by the rivals, because their survival had ultimately resulted in a far greater destruction of Hindu shrines and the setting up of abattoirs all over the country.

And he had a "final word" of indictment for those non-Hindus who saw cow slaughter as a religious duty. He said: Hindus were naïve in their worship, but they weren't cruel. Those who cut down the animal as part of their dharma were not only naïve but brutal in their religious zealotry, he said, and added that they had no right to ridicule Hindus for their beliefs. In such slaughter, Savarkar saw excessive barbarism, ingratitude and an asuric (demonic) instinct. He urged such non-Hindus to give up their "cow hate" and take up "cow care."

Even if firmly situated within the Hindutva framework and calling openly for a Hindu Rashtra, this is a surprisingly complex and often apparently contradictory opinion on a subject highly sensitive in today's India. But Savarkar's view is also perhaps unique in that both the gaurakshaks and the Youth Congress's public slaughterers of a calf in Kerala might wonder what exactly to make of him.

Vinayak Damodar Savarkar, as the fiery Indian revolutionary from Nashik, had come to be then known after his attempted escape from British captivity in Marseilles and more than a decade in the Andamans' Cellular Jail, responded to this assertion. He wrote: "If the cow's a mother to anybody at all, it's the bullock. Hindutva, if it has to sustain itself on a cow's legs, will come crashing down at the slightest sign of a crisis."

3

Savarkar on Cow Worship

Savarkar held radical views even on matters such as cow-worship. He wrote, "Animals such as the cow and buffalo and trees such as banyan and peepal are useful to man. Hence, we are fond of them; to that extent we might even consider them worthy of worship. Their protection, sustenance and well-being is our duty, in that sense alone it is also our dharma!"

At the same time, he cautioned that if the "animal or tree becomes a source of trouble to mankind, it ceases to be worthy of sustenance or protection and as such its destruction is in humanitarian or national interests, and it becomes a human or national dharma. When humanitarian interests are not served and in fact harmed by the cow, and when humanism is shamed, self-defeating extreme cow protection should be rejected."

4

Savarkar on Cow-Vigilantism

He also asserted that while he held the cow as a beautiful creature, protecting it and not worshipping it as a goddess was his belief, "Elevating an animal that eats garbage and sits in its own excreta to the position of a goddess, was insulting both humanity and divinity," Savarkar said.

"We become God we worship and hence, Hindutva's icon should be the Narasimha or fierce man-lion and not the docile cow," wrote Savarkar.

Savarkar concludes the essay saying, "I am no enemy of the cow. I have only criticized the false notions and tendencies involved in cow worship with the aim of removing the chaff and preserving the essence so that genuine cow protection may be better achieved. Without spreading religious superstition, let the movement for cow protection be based and popularized on clear-cut economic and scientific principles. A worshipful attitude is undoubtedly necessary for protection. But it is improper to forget the duty of cow protection and indulge only in worship."

Just like he gave a call to the Hindu community to give up these superstitions, he exhorted the Muslims too to reform themselves with time and "abandon the belief that not even a word in the Quran can be questioned because it is the eternal message of God, even as you maintain respect for the Quran."

Elaborating, Savarkar said that the norms that seemed feasible to an oppressed but backward people in Arabia at a time of civil strife could not be accepted as an eternal way of life. The Muslims must "accept the habit of sticking to only that, which is relevant in the modern age," he said.

5

Savarkar's Views on Vegetarianism

Savarkar had no qualms about vegetarianism like several Brahmins of the time. In October 1906, he met young Mohandas Karamchand Gandhi for the first time when the latter came to the India House in London where Savarkar and other revolutionaries lived. Savarkar was busy cooking his meals when Gandhi joined him to engage in a political discussion. Cutting him short, Savarkar asked him to first eat. Gandhi was quite horrified to see the Chitpawan Brahmin cooking prawns, and being a staunch vegetarian, he (Gandhi) refused to partake.

Savarkar apparently mocked at him and retorted, "Well, if you can not eat with us, how on earth are you going to work with us? Moreover, this is just boiled fish, while we want people who are ready to eat the British alive." This was obviously not a great first meeting and their differences only widened with time. As Savarkar's political thoughts matured during his long years of incarceration, he penned some poetic essays on the abhorrent practice of the caste system and untouchability, and how these sapped the very vitals of the nation.

6

Savarkar's Views on Castes

Despite being born in an orthodox and religious Chitpavan Brahmin community, right from childhood Savarkar despised the caste system. He developed close kinship with children from various castes and strata of society and also dined at their homes. He was among the few Brahmins of the time who took to sea-travel to London for his education, at a time when most members of his community forbade it due to the fear of a loss of caste.

Savakar was the pioneer of the vision of a casteless India. He advocated strongly for total, complete and unconditional eradication of casts system. He imagined a situation when these castes were not issues of the political discourse popularized by either Gandhi or Ambedkar. In his essay titled *Seven Shackles of the Hindu Society*, Savarkar says that heredity is not a determinant of talent and intellect and an individual's environment is what shapes his character and conduct. He takes a high radical stand against those scriptural injunctions, including the Manusmriti that advocated castes.

To Savarkar's view, the scriptures that were self-contradicting were created by human beings and were relevant in a particular context and in a particular society. "They need to evolve or be discarded as society moves ahead," he said. He viewed the caste system as an evil that splintered and disunited Hindu society, making it susceptible to attacks and conversions by other groups.

The seven fetters that he advocated a complete dismantling of were:

1. *Vedoktabandi:* Exclusivity of access to Vedic literature and rituals to only the Brahmin community.
2. *Vyavasaayabandi:* Choice of a profession an individual chooses must be entirely his and based on his aptitude and capability and not on one's birth.
3. *Sparshabandi:*Untouchability that he considered a sin and a

blot on society.

4. *Samudrabandi:* Loss of caste on foreign travel or crossing the seas.

5. *Shuddhibandi:* Disallowing reconversions to Hinduism. "I have nothing," he said, "against those who convert to another faith by sheer conviction. But such examples are rare. Why should we not allow the enhancement of our (Hindu) members due to some antiquated idea that does not even have any scriptural sanction that we cannot convert to Hinduism?"

6. *Rotibandi:* Prohibition on inter-caste dining.

7. *Betibandi*: Prohibition on inter-caste marriage.

7

Savarkar on Social Reforms

Calling for a reinterpretation of the chaturvarna or four Varna system based on Lord Krishna's assertion in the Bhagavad Gita that it was He, who created the four varnas, Savarkar writes, "Different human beings have different qualities and virtues. All that Lord Krishna says is—I create human beings who are different in nature, character, virtues and values—yet, good or bad, they are all my creation alone. Nowhere in this declaration does he state that I also make those virtues hereditary for the person's successive generation. We are all shudras at birth. As life progresses, we attain qualities, education, and virtues to graduate to various levels of consciousness and thinking—that is the fundamental concept behind the four Varna system." Savarkar asserted strongly that the Varna system was not a part of Sanatan Dharma. Sanatan are those lofty ideals and beliefs. He said, "Predate and time are indestructible, whereas social practices such as caste system, opposition to widow remarriage or vegetarianism are man-made social practices and rituals that can easily be dismantled depending on the needs of the society."

To further these beliefs, Savarkar advocated social reforms on a large scale during his incarceration in Ratnagiri from 1924 to 1937. Among his measures that earned the ire of the local Brahmin community were the advocacy of large scale inter-caste dining and the establishment of a PatitPavan (literally meaning the protector of the fallen) temple that allowed entry to members of all castes for community prayers.

8

Savarkar as an Atheist

Savarkar was an atheist. When he was the Hindu Mahasabha president, he used to give lectures on why there is no God. So the question was, how can you be a Hindu communalist and yet be an atheist? So, he coined the concept of Hindutva. He described Hindus as those whose holy places are in India. Which means Muslims and Christians are out of the pale of Hindutva. Consequently, Savarkar gave a tradition of communalism.

In 1937, he even adduced the theory of two nations. The interesting thing is, very few people knew about his Hindutva part. Once Gandhiji became aware of this, he said his politics and that of Savarkar were totally different. Neither his Hindutva aspect nor his apology aspect was known largely. People knew about his involvement in the assassination of Gandhiji for which the court said, "Savarkar was not guilty." But, people did not realize it.

It was not important who Gandhiji's assassin was. It was Savarkar and Golwalkar who declared Gandhi as anti-Hindu. They carried out a campaign that Gandhi was anti-national and anti-Hindu and that he (Gandhi) was a lover of Islam and wanted India Islamised. His non-violence meant disarming the Hindus.

The hatred against Gandhiji was spread by the Rashtriya Swayamsevak Sangh and Savarkar who was an important leader of the Hindu Mahasabha. The important point is not whether Savarkar organized the conspiracy to assassinate Gandhiji. What is important is Savarkar was the theoretician of Hindutva, its ideology.

9

Savarkar: A True Nationalist

An undying nationalist who relied on logic and scientific temper, Savarkar decried Gandhi's attempt to attribute the devastating earthquake in Bihar in 1934 to God's curse on Indians for practicing untouchability.

"It is our misfortune in India," he said, "that even someone as influential as Gandhi ji invokes his "inner voice" to attribute the recent massive Bihar earthquake as God's punishment for the barbaric caste system! I still wait to hear what the Mahatma's inner voice will tell us about why Quetta was rocked by an earthquake!"

A staunch advocate of a capitalist, market-driven, mechanized society, Savarkar wrote as early as in the 1930s about scientific temper alone being the foundation of a modern and prosperous India.

"It is through science, modern thoughts and industrialization and not by spinning wheels," he held, "that we can ensure that every man and woman in India will have a job to do, food to eat, clothes to wear and a happy life to lead."

His views that were radical and far ahead of his times caused friction even within members of the Hindutva fold, such as the Rashtriya Swayamsevak Sangh (RSS) that held more orthodox views on such matters. This was possibly why Savarkar stayed away from the RSS, even though his elder brother Ganesh Damodar was among the founding members of the Sangh, along with K.B. Hedgewar.

A retrospective unbiased and clinical analysis of Savarkar's writings on society, science, economy and foreign affairs show how so many of his predictions eventually turned out to be true. If the timelessness and relevance of a leader's thoughts are the litmus of his greatness, Savarkar certainly was one.

10

Savarkar as a Role Model

When we were young, he, Savarkar, was a role model. We respected and honoured him from the point of view of commitment, sacrifice and courage during India's freedom struggle. But Savarkar broke down in jail (*he was transported to the Andamans for life imprisonment under the British government*) and a person who breaks down cannot be seen as a role model for the Indian youth.

What Savarkar did was to take the opposite direction. He apologized. He begged for clemency from the British government. He told the British if they released him, he would tell his comrades that the path he was following was wrong. Therefore, Savarkar's breaking down means he can no longer be seen as a role model.

11

Savarkar Denied as a Role Model

There was an ongoing anti-imperialist struggle, and Savarkar was a part of it. He wrote a book called *1857 - War of Independence*. One of the things he emphasized was Hindu-Muslim unity in India, because he was aware of the fact that one could not fight British imperialism with one-fourth of the population alienated. Even at that time, he had certain anti-Muslim prejudice. Our national movement from the very first day from 1870 onwards favoured unity of all castes, classes and all areas because unless the Indian people were united, it was impossible to strive for independence against the mighty British Empire.

Now, what did Savarkar do when he was released? Firstly, he accepted humiliating conditions including his non-participation in politics. That is not so bad because that doesn't make him a villain. But even after all this; he still wanted to be a prominent person. How can he be a prominent person (*in those times*) and not be an anti-imperialist?

So, Savarkar chose to become a communalist. This was the only political channel open to him. By the way, it was the reason why Jinnah turned to virulent communalism.

12

Savarkar on Hindutva

Savarkar in his important work, *Hindutva: Who is a Hindu,* developed the core of his philosophy on the concept of Hindutva. According to Savarkar, Hindutva was not a word but a history. It was not only a history of the spiritual or religious life of the Indian people but a history of the entire civilization.

In order to make Hindutva a grand concept, Savarkar held that by an 'ism' it was generally meant a theory or a code more or less based on spiritual or religious dogma or system. In order to investigate into the essential significance of Hindutva, Savarkar did not primarily concern himself with any particular theocratic or religious dogma or creed. He held that had the linguistic usage not stood in the way, then 'Hinduness' would have certainly been a better word than 'Hinduism' as a close parallel to Hindutva.

Savarkar was of the opinion that Hindutva embraced all the departments of thought and activity of the whole being of the Hindu race. He held that to understand the significance of this term Hindutva, one should understand first the essential meaning of the word 'Hindu' itself and 'realize how it came to exercise such imperial sway over the hearts of millions of mankind and won a loving allegiance from the bravest and best of them.' However, Savarkar felt it imperative to point out that he was by no means attempting a definition or even a description of the more limited, less satisfactory and essentially sectarian term 'Hinduism'. Savarkar admitted that the concern of the theoreticians had been more with what would have been or what should be. Savarkar was not opposed to this kind of inquiry which in his opinion was "necessary and at times more stimulating."

However, he was more emphatic on the point that one should first get a firm hold of what actually was in his own words: "We must try, therefore, to be on our guard so that in our attempt to determine the essentials of Hindutva, we be guided entirely by the actual contents of the word as it stands at present. So although the root meaning of the word Hindu like the sister epithet Hindi may mean only an Indian, yet as it is, we would be straining the usage of words too much - we fear, to the point of breaking - if we call a Mohammedan a Hindu because of his being a resident of India."

However, Savarkar did not rule it out as impossibility. On the contrary, he held that at some future time the word Hindu might come to indicate a citizen of India and nothing else. He was of the opinion that such a historical situation would only arise when 'all cultural and religious bigotry had disbanded its forces pledged to aggresive egoism'. "For although the first requisite of Hindutva is that he be a citizen of Hindusthan either

by himself or through his forefathers, yet it is not the only requisite qualification of it,

as the term Hindu has come to mean much more than its geographical significance."

According to Savarkar every person is a Hindu who regarded this land as his 'Fatherland' as well as his 'Holyland', i.e. the land of the origin of his religion. Savarkar held that the followers of 'Vaidicism, Sanatanism, Jainism, Buddhism, Lingaitism, Sikhism, the Arya Samaj, the Brahmo Samaj, the Dev Samaj, the PrarthanaSamaj and such other religions of Hindusthani origin', were Hindus and constituted 'Hindudom.'

Savarkar opined that the Indian Muslims, Christians, Jews, Parsees were excluded from the right to claim themselves as Hindus, in spite of India being their Fatherland. Similarly, though the Japanese, the Chinese and other nationals considered India as their 'Holyland', yet they were not considered as Hindu people because this land was not their 'Fatherland', i.e., the land of their forefathers. So, according to Savarkar, a person would be considered Hindu, i.e., a normal citizen of Hindusthan, if he or she fulfilled two criteria of Hindutva.

Savarkar defined Hindutva as not only the spiritual or religious history of the Hindus, but the history in full pervasion. Hinduism was only a derivative, a fraction, a part of Hindutva. He observed that Hindutva was not particularly theocratic, a religious dogma or a creed. It embraced all the departments of thought and activity of the whole being of the Hindu race. Savarkar stated that: "Forty centuries, if not more, had been at work to mould it as it is. Prophets and poets, lawyers and lawgivers, heroes and historians, have thought, lived, fought and died just to have it spelled thus." Savarkar's main argument in his book *Hindutva* was that the Aryans who settled in India at the dawn of history already formed a nation later embodied in the Hindus. Their Hindutva, according to him, rested on three pillars:

geographical unity, racial features and a common culture. Savarkar minimized the importance of religious criterion in the definition of a Hindu by claiming that Hinduism was only one of the attributes of 'Hinduness. The notion of territory was at the heart of Savarkar's ideological construct but not in the same way as in the Universalist conceptions of nationalism; for Savarkar, the territory of India could not be dissociated from Hindu culture and the Hindu people. In his eyes, Hindus were pre-eminently the descendants of the 'intrepid Aryans (who) made it (the subcontinent) their home and lighted the first sacrificial fire on the bank of the Indus', a river which he considered to be the western border of the Hindu nation. Savarkar's view that the Indus was the frontier of the Hindu nation was part of a broader reinterpretation of the word 'Hindu' or 'Sindhu', the letters 'h' and 's' being interchangable in Sanskrit : "Sindhu in Sanskrit does not only mean the Indus but also the sea—which girdles the southern peninsula—so that this one word Sindhu points out almost all frontiers of the land at a single stroke and so the epithet Sindhusthan calls up the image of our whole Motherland: the land that is between Sindhu and Sindhu—from the Indus to the sea."

For Savarkar a Hindu was, therefore, an inhabitant of the zone between the rivers, the seas and the Himalayas so strongly entrenched that no other country in the world is so

perfectly designed by the fingers of nature as a geographical unit. This was why, in the Vedic era, the first Aryans developed there 'the sense of unity of a people' and even a 'sense of nationality'. Here we perceive an ethnic logic, i.e., the enclosed character of Hindusthan was described as the factor that determined the social unity of a population marked by intermarriage. Savarkar emphasized that his was not a territorial conception of nationalism as the stress on geographical unity might have suggested. Savarkar held that the Hindus were not merely the citizens of the Indian state because they were united not merely by the bonds of love they bore to a common motherland but also by the bonds of a common blood. They were not only a nation but a race—jati. According to Savarkar, a race or jati was determined by a common origin.

But, nowadays, they say that Hindutva is nothing but Hindu communalism. The word 'communalism' has become so dirty in our country that even communalists don't call themselves communalists. The votaries of Hindutva have shifted from their initial stance on Hindu rashtra. Moreover, it lacks intellectuality of any standing. Savarkar was supporting Nazism and Fascism. That is because of his anti-Muslim stand. He felt that Hindus were in majority and, therefore, they should rule the Muslims like that Hitler was doing to the Jews.

13

Savarkar's Hindutva Ideology Derailed Freedom Movement

The sectarian mindset, which eventually culminated into the articulation of Hindutva ideology, was evident — as Jyotirmaya Sharma has demonstrated in *Hindutva: Exploring the Idea of Hindu Nationalism* —in the early Savarkar, that too from a tender age. Only a boy of 12, Savarkar, leading a pack of his schoolmates, attacked a mosque in the aftermath of the Hindu-Muslim riots in Bombay and Pune in 1894-95. Holding back the Muslim boys of the village using "knives, pins and foot rulers", Savarkar and his friends mounted their attack, "Showering stones on the mosque, shattering its windows and tiles." Recollecting the incident, he later wrote, "We vandalised the mosque to our heart's consent and raised the flag of our bravery on it." When the news of Hindus killing Muslims in the riots and its aftermath reached him, little Savarkar and his friends "would dance with joy."

The sectarian nature of Savarkar's social and political thinking not only bred in him a deep-rooted resentment against Muslims but also clouded his understanding of historical events, leading him to perceive the 1857 War of Indian Independence as retaliation by Hindus and Muslims against Christianity, in response to Britain's efforts to Christianise India. In his book, *The War of Independence of 1857,* published during his revolutionary days, years before he had declared his loyalty to the British government, Savarkar wrote, quoting Justin McCarthy, "The Mahomedan and the Hindu forgot their old religious antipathies to join against the Christian."

What was to stop the British government, which had passed a law against the practice of Sati (widow burning), from meddling further with Hindu customs by passing a law against idolatry, he asked. After all, "The English hated idolatry as much as they did suttee." Describing a process he perceived to is the destruction of Hinduism and Islam in India, Savarkar wrote in his book:

"The Sirkar (government) had already begun to pass one law after another to destroy the foundations of the Hindu and Mahomedan religions. Railways had already been constructed, and carriages had been built in such a way as to offend the caste prejudices of the Hindus. The larger mission schools were being helped with huge grants from the Sirkar. Lord Canning himself distributed thousands of Rupees to every mission, and from this fact, it is clear that the wish was strong in the heart of Lord Canning that all India should be Christian."

The sepoys, according to Savarkar, were the primary targets in this mission to spread Christianity in India. "If any Sepoy accepted the Christian religion, he was praised loudly and treated honourably; and this Sepoy was promoted in the ranks and his salary increased, in the face of the superior merits of the other Sepoys!"

"Everywhere", he argued, "there was a strong conviction that the Government had determined to destroy the religions of the country and make Christianity the paramount religion of the land". By thus giving religion an unwarranted centrality in his analysis of the causes of the rebellion, Savarkar, says Jyotirmaya Sharma, expressed jubilation in his accounts of the rebellion "at every instance of a church being felled, a cross being smashed and every Christian being 'sliced'."

While the seeds of communalism had been sown in his mind at a very young age, the poison fruit of Hindutva ideology was to blossom only in his late 20s, after Savarkar's will to fight the British (or the Christians, as he often referred to them in his book on the 1857 uprising) had been defeated during his imprisonment. It was during his last few years of imprisonment that Savarkar first articulated the concept of Hindutva in his book, Essentials of Hindutva, which was published in 1923 and reprinted with a new title as "*Hindutva: Who Is a Hindu?*" in 1928. This ideology was a deeply divisive one which had the potential to distract attention from the British and cast it on Muslims instead.

While he was careful to specify that Hindutva, or 'Hinduness', was different from Hinduism and encompassed a wide range of cultures including, among others, the "Sanatanists, Satnamis, Sikhs, Aryas, Anaryas, Marathas and Madrasis, Brahmins and Panchamas", he nonetheless made it a point to warn that it "would be straining the usage of words too much – we fear, to the point of breaking – if we call a Mohammedan a Hindu because of his being a resident of India."

"Mohammedan or Christian communities", he argued, "possess all the essential qualifications of Hindutva but one and that is that they do not look upon India as their Holyland." A cohesive nation, according to Savarkar, can ideally be built only by those people who inhabit a country which is not only the land of their forefathers, but "also the land of their Gods and Angels, of Seers and Prophets; the scenes of whose history are also the scenes of their mythology."

The love and loyalty of Muslims, he warned, "Is, and must necessarily be divided between the land of their birth and the land of their Prophets. Mohammedans would naturally set the interests of their Holyland above those of their Motherland." One might wonder whether this line of reasoning implies that Muslims cannot be nationals of Pakistan or Afghanistan either, because they would place the interests of Saudi Arabia, wherein lie Mecca and Madina, above the interests of their own country.

Back in the 1920s, the damage that could be done to the freedom movement by his ideology did not fail to come to the notice of the colonial government. Even though Savarkar was released on condition that he should not participate in political activities, he was allowed by the British to organize the Ratnagiri Mahasabha, which undertook what is in today's lingo called "Ghar Wapsi" and played music in front of mosques while prayers were on.

In spite of the blanket ban on political participation, Shamsul Islam pointed out: "The British rulers naturally overlooked these political activities as the future of colonial rule in India rested on the communal divide and Savarkar was leaving no stone unturned in aggravating the Hindu-Muslim divide."

14

Savarkar: A Brave Heart

He arrived in the Andaman Islands in July 1911 where he stayed until 1921, when he was moved to Ratnagiri, Bombay Presidency, where he was imprisoned until 1924 and interned until 1937. During his imprisonment, he wrote *Hindutva: What is a Hindu?* After 1937, Savarkar continued his anti-Muslim, anti-British politics and became the ideological alternative to Gandhi's non-violence politics, as President of the right-wing Hindu Mahasabha. He remained a huge political influence until his death in Bombay in 1966.

In a letter dated November 14, 1913, Savarkar said: "If the government in their manifold beneficence and mercy release me, I for one cannot but be the staunchest advocate of constitutional progress and loyalty to the English government which is the foremost condition of that progress. Moreover, my conversion to the constitutional line would bring back all those misled young men in India and abroad who were once looking up to me as their guide. The Mighty alone can afford to be merciful and, therefore, where else can the prodigal son return but to the parental doors of the government?"

Conditions in the prison were no doubt harsh, but a few of the prisoners did face them courageously. Savarkar was not one of them. A brief account of these long-forgotten heroes is in order:

Nand Gopal, Editor of Swaraj (Allahabad), was sentenced to life for seditious writing. His successful passive resistance to the punishment of working in the oil mill led to the first strike of the political prisoners. At about the same time, Hotilal, also associated with Swaraj, successfully smuggled to India his letter detailing the atrocities on them. This letter, published by Surendranath Banerjee in *The Bengali,* gave a glimpse of the prison life in the Andamans and created uproar in the country.

There was another general strike in the prison during which 16-year-old Nand Gopal, among others, risked caning and death to continue with a hunger strike. Ultimately, Savarkar started a hunger strike to force Nand Gopal to back off. Savarkar's advice to Nand Gopal revealed his mindset: "Do not die like a woman; if you must need, die fighting like a hero. Kill your enemy and then take leave of this world."

Trailokyanath Chakravarthi, who was transported to the Andamans as a prisoner in 1916, gives an interesting account of the reluctance of the Savarkar brothers (and a few other senior leaders) to join them in their civil disobedience movement. They were reluctant, according to Chakravarthi, because "they had wrung some concessions and privileges after a hard fight". Justifying his behaviour, Savarkar said: "And now to be put again in chains and solitary confinement, to go back to bad food and expose ourselves to caning, was to expect too much from us. The last and the most important reasons for my abstaining from it was that I would have forfeited thereby my right of sending a letter to India." and his various appeals for clemency suggest a possible breakdown of his resolve.

There has been a lot of controversy regarding Savarkar's position on the two-nation theory. In October 1938, he dropped strong hints about the impossibility of the co-existence of Hindus and Muslims: "A nation is formed by a majority living therein. What did the Jews do in Germany? They being in minority were driven out from Germany." And in July 1939, he said: "Nationality did not depend so much on a common geographical area as on unity of thought, religion, language and culture. For this reason the Germans and the Jews could not be regarded as a nation." Later that year, in the 21st session of the Hindu Mahasabha, he laid all doubts to rest with his comment: "The Indian Muslims are on the whole more inclined to identify themselves and their interests with Muslims outside India than Hindus who live next door, like Jews in Germany." He justified his assertion when he said: But besides culture the tie of common holyland has at times proved stronger than the chains of a Motherland. Look at the Mohammedans. Mecca to them is a stronger reality than Delhi or Agra. Some of them do not make any secret of being bound to sacrifice all India if that be to the glory of Islam or could save the city of their Prophet. History is too full of examples of such desertions. The crusades again attest to the wonderful influence that a common holyland exercises over peoples widely separated in race, nationality and language, to bind and hold them together."

Savarkar defines a Hindu as one "who regards this land of Bharatvarsha, from the Indus to the Seas as his Father-Land as well as his Holy-Land that is the cradle land of his religion". He said: "So with the Hindus, they being the people, whose past, present and future are most closely bound with the soil of Hindusthan as Pitribhu (fatherland), as Punyabhu (holyland), they constitute the foundation, the bedrock, the reserved forces of the Indian state. Therefore, even from the point of Indian nationality, must ye, O Hindus, consolidate and strengthen Hindu nationality; not to give wanton offence to any of our non-Hindu compatriots, in fact to any one in the world but in just and urgent defence of our race and land; to render it impossible for others to betray her to or subject her to unprovoked attack by any of those 'Pan-isms' that are struggling forth from continent to continent." The obvious conclusions are:

1. Since Muslims and Hindus do not possess "unity of thought, religion, language and culture", they cannot co-exist.

2. Muslims' allegiance to India is weaker than their allegiance to their holy-land (which lies outside of India), and so their patriotism is suspected.

3. Being the minority, Muslims need to be at the mercy of Hindus. Getting rid of Muslims is also justified, for that was what the Germans did to the Jews.

Savarkar: His Two-Nation Theory

Savarkar's support for the two-nation theory is confirmed by his assertion: "I have no quarrel with Mr. Jinnah's two-nation theory. We, Hindus, are a nation by ourselves and it is a historical fact that Hindus and Muslims are two nations." This position is easy to understand, for Savarkar maintained that India bereft of Muslims was relatively inert to sabotage from within. Savarkar's obsession with the dictatorship of the majority is evident from what he proclaimed in favour of a Jewish state despite his support to the Holocaust. He said, "If the Zionists' dreams are ever realized — if Palestine becomes a Jewish state and it will gladden us almost as much as our Jewish friends."

15

Savarkar's Pleadings for Mercy

Barely a month into the hardships of prison, Savarkar wrote his first mercy petition which was rejected in 1911. The second mercy petition which he wrote in 1913 starts with bitter complaints about other convicts from his party receiving better treatment than him:

"When I came here in 1911 June, I was along with the rest of the convicts of my party taken to the office of the Chief Commissioner. There I was classed as "D" meaning dangerous prisoner; the rest of the convicts were not classed as "D". Then I had to pass full 6 months in solitary confinement. The other convicts had not. Although my conduct during all the time was exceptionally good, still at the end of these six months, I was not sent out of the jail; though the other convicts who came with me were.

For those who are term convicts, the thing is different, but Sir, I have 50 years staring me in the face! How can I pull up moral energy enough to pass them in close confinement when even those concessions which the vilest of convicts can claim to smoothen their life are denied to me?"

Then, after confessing that he was misguided into taking the revolutionary road because of the "excited and hopeless situation of India in 1906-1907", he concluded his November 14, 1913 petition by assuring the British of his conscientious conversion. "If the government in their manifold beneficence and mercy release me," he wrote, "I for one cannot but be *the staunchest advocate of loyalty to the English government.*"

"Moreover," he went on to say, making an offer which few freedom fighters could even think of making, "my conversion to the constitutional line would bring back all those misled young men in India and abroad who were once looking up to me as their guide. I am ready to serve the Government in any capacity they like, for as my conversion is conscientious. The Mighty alone can afford to be merciful, and therefore, where else can the prodigal son return but to the paternal doors of the government?"

In his fourth mercy petition, dated March 30, 1920, Savarkar told the British that under the threat of an invasion from the north by the "fanatic hordes of Asia" who were posing as "friends", he was convinced that "every intelligent lover of India would heartily and loyally co-operate with the British people in the interests of India herself."

After reassuring the colonial government that he was trying his "humble best to render the hands of the British dominion a bond of love and respect," Savarkar went on to exalt the English empire: "Such an Empire as is foreshadowed in the Proclamation, wins my hearty adherence". "But", he added:

"If the Government wants further security from me, then I and my brother are perfectly willing to give a pledge of not participating in politics for a definite and reasonable period that the Government would indicate. This or any pledge, e.g., of remaining in a particular province or reporting our movements to the police for a definite period after our release – any such reasonable conditions meant genuinely to ensure the safety of the State would be gladly accepted by me and my brother."

Finally, after spending ten years in the cellular jail and writing many mercy petitions, Savarkar, along with his brother, was shifted to a prison in Ratnagiri in 1921, before his subsequent release in 1924 on the condition of the confinement of his movements to the Ratnagiri district and his non-participation in political activities. These restrictions were lifted only in 1937.

Most importantly, in this petition, he explicitly stated that, "If the Government thinks that it is only to effect my own release that I pen this; or if my name constitutes the chief obstacle in the granting of such an amnesty; then let the Government omit my name in their amnesty and release all the rest; that would give me as great a satisfaction as my own release would do."

It was only when the Cellular Jail was about to be closed, then the British decided to deport Savarkar to the Ratnagiri Prison in May 1921.

16

Savarkar's Petitions are Just and Fair

The freedom fighter Vinayak Damodar Savarkar had apologized to the British to be released from jail. In the five years that Savarkar spent in London as a law student, he galvanized the revolutionary movement that sought total and complete freedom from British rule. From India to Europe, and even America, a network of bravehearts guided by him, made contacts with Irish, French, Italian, Russian and American leaders, revolutionaries and the press to bring British India to the forefront of global discourse. No doubt, the British government categorized him as one of the most dangerous seditionists. Under an unfair Fugitive Offenders Act (FOA) of 1881 that did not apply to him because he was a bonafide student in London and not a fugitive, Savarkar was deported to India and tried with no right to appeal or defence. He was slapped with two life imprisonments, totalling 50 years, to rot in the Cellular Jail of the Andamans along with his elder brother Ganesh Damodar Savarkar. The British documents speak of how petrified they were of his very presence and hence wanted him as far away from the Indian mainland as possible.

In the Cellular Jail, he was meted the worst kind of punishments. Fettered in chains, flogged, condemned to six months of solitary confinement, made to extract oil all day being tied to the mill like a bullock, punished with standing handcuffs for days on end, lack of the most basic human needs such as toilets or water and fed with foul food that had pieces of insects and reptiles — it was truly a devil's island.

By 1913, Savarkar and several other prisoners began hunger strikes and non-cooperation in jail to protest against this inhuman treatment. The rest of India was blissfully unaware of the tortures their compatriots faced in KaalaPani. Hence, articles were leaked out for publication in Indian newspapers. Savarkar's clandestine attempts to start bomb manufacturing in Port Blair alarmed the authorities. Finally, in October 1913, Sir Reginald H. Craddock, home member of the government of India, decided to visit the Cellular Jail and interview some of the political prisoners to ascertain their grievances. Savarkar and other political prisoners — Barin Ghose, Nand Gopal, Hrishikesh Kanjilal and Sudhir Kumar Sarkar were interviewed and allowed to submit petitions. This process was a legitimate tool available for all political prisoners in British India, just like the opportunity of defending oneself in court through the agency of a lawyer was. As a barrister, Savarkar knew the law and wished to utilize all provisions under it to free himself or alleviate his situation in prison. Savarkar often advised other political prisoners too that the primary duty of a revolutionary was to free himself from the British clutches so as to return to the freedom struggle and in service of the motherland.

In his petition dated 14 November 1913 to Craddock, Savarkar argued that while common convicts of rape, murder, theft and other crimes were given promotions on the basis of their good conduct or let out into the settlement for work after 6-18 months, such provisions were not available for him as he was a 'special class prisoner'. But when he asked for better food or treatment, he was denied those on the basis of being an 'ordinary convict'. Had he been a political prisoner in an Indian jail, he would have earned remission or could write more than just the single annual letter and meeting with his family that he was allowed. This dichotomy disadvantaged him on both fronts.

By 1909, the Morley-Minto Reforms brought in a slew of greater opportunities for Indians to participate in councils and education. Hence, Savarkar alludes in his petition that the need to pick up the gun no longer remained, and he was happy to join mainstream politics and work with the government towards greater constitutional participation for Indians. "I am not asking for any preferential treatment, he said "though I believe as a political prisoner even that could have been expected in any civilized administration in the Independent nations of the world; but only for the concessions and favour that are shown even to the most depraved of convicts and habitual criminals?" It was almost an indirect mockery of British India being uncivilized.

Ironically those who castigate Savarkar for the petitions are the same human rights activists who advocate the cause of the likes of Kasab, Yakub Memon, and the Naxals and their intellectual fountain heads. The last line of this petition that draws controversy is open to interpretation: "The mighty alone can afford to be merciful and, therefore, where else can the prodigal son return, but to the parental doors of the Government?" Being a Biblical reference, it can well be said that he was appealing to the religious sentiments of his incarcerations. Selective quoting of just a few lines of this petition, without looking at it completely or in context, is intellectually just and fair.

Interestingly, on his way back to India, Craddock wrote his report onboard the ship where he said that Savarkar "cannot be said to express any regret or repentance" for whatever he did. "So important a leader he is!" Craddock noted, "that the European section of the Indian anarchists would plot for his escape which would before long be organized. If he were allowed outside the Cellular Jail in the Andamans, his escape would be certain. His friends could easily charter a steamer to lie off one of the islands and a little money distributed locally would do the rest." The government obviously rejected his petition and nothing changed for Savarkar.

With the outbreak of the First World War, Savarkar filed another petition in October, 1914 offering to "volunteer to do any service in the present War that the Indian government thinks fit to demand". In the same petition, he also requested a general release of "all those prisoners who had been convicted for committing political offences in India". This was being done in many British colonies.

Interestingly, the Indian National Congress openly supported Britain during this crucial period. When the War broke out, Mahatma Gandhi was in England where he began organizing a medical corps similar to the force he had led in aid of the British during the World War and even won a gold medal for loyalty. In a circular dated 22 September 1914, he called for recruitment to his Field Ambulance Training Corps. On his return to India in January 1915, Gandhi Ji offered unconditional support for British efforts in the War and believed that it was not a good time to embarrass Britain or take advantage of her troubled situation to further the Indian liberation cause.

"England's need," he said, "should not be turned into our opportunity and that it was more becoming and far-sighted not to press our demands while the war lasted." Marching from village to village in Gujarat, he recruited volunteers to assist the British in the War. How was this any different from Savarkar's 1914 petition then?

In his next petition on 5 October, 1917 to the Secretary of State to India, Edwin Samuel Montagu, Savarkar referred to the Montague-Chelmsford Reforms that were on the anvil promising limited self-government and a bicameral legislature to Indians. He strongly advocated the grant of home rule to India and her becoming an autonomous partner of the Commonwealth. "When there was no Constitution", he postulated, "It seemed a mockery to talk of constitutional movements. But now if a Constitution exists, and Home Rule is decidedly such, then so much political, social, economic, and educational work is to be done and could be constitutionally done that the Government may securely rest satisfied that none of the political prisoners would choose to face untold suffering by resorting to underground methods for sheer amusement." Invoking international precedents in Russia, France, Ireland, Transvaal and Austria where amnesty was becoming the general principle, he argued his case like a good lawyer.

Most importantly, in this petition he explicitly stated that, "if the Government thinks that it is only to effect my own release that I pen this; or if my name constitutes the chief obstacle in the granting of such an amnesty; then let the Government omit my name in their amnesty and release all the rest; that would give me as great a satisfaction as my own release would do."Can these be the words of a coward or an opportunist British stooge?

With the end of the War, Emperor George V's royal proclamation granted a wholesale amnesty to all political prisoners lodged across India and the Andamans. BarinGhose, Trailokya Nath Chakravarti, Hemachandra Das, Sachindra Nath Sanyal, Parmanand and others in Cellular Jail, were released with a pledge to not participate in politics for a stipulated time. Congress workers who had been arrested after the non-cooperation movement of 1919 were also released on this principle. However, the same benefits were not accrued to Savarkar and his elder brother. Sachindra Nath Sanyal in his memoirs talks about sending an identical petition as Savarkar and being released while the latter was still imprisoned since the government feared that their release would rekindle the fizzled revolutionary movement in Maharashtra that they had spearheaded through their secret organization — Abhinav Bharat.

Naturally, Savarkar appealed against injustice through his petitions. In none of his petitions does he ever say— he was apologetic of his revolutionary past.

It was only when the Cellular Jail was about to be closed that the British decided to deport Savarkar to the Ratnagiri Prison in May 1921. By then Savarkar had managed to accomplish significant prison reforms at Port Blair—from setting up a library, to education for convicts and stopping all forcible conversions. To his horror, he discovered that these benefits that he strove to get in the Andamans were all stripped off him at Ratnagiri and he was back to where he began his prison journey. This broke his will and he wrote unabashedly in his memoirs, *My Transportation for Life*, that this was the third time (the first two being in Port Blair) that he seriously contemplated suicide as he found his situation hopeless. It was immense resilience and inner strength that he drew to nip those thoughts, unlike several other political prisoners who hanged themselves to the ceilings of their tiny cells or went insane. In such a state of mind, his petition of 19 August 1921 indicates the spirit of a broken and dejected man, considering even political renunciation.

It was three years later on 6 January 1924 that Savarkar was released from prison but kept under strict surveillance within the frontiers of Ratnagiri district and debarred from political activity. He spent the next 13 years of his life this way. But it did not stop him from beginning a series of social reforms in Ratnagiri to break the caste system. Long before the Harijan movement or B. R. Ambedkar's clarion call, Savarkar championed inter-caste dining and also built a PatitPavan temple in Ratnagiri that allowed entry to all castes. An objective assessment of a much-maligned Vinayak Damodar Savarkar calls for many questions.

The future events in his long and distinguished political career actually validate the allegation of his willingness to acquiesce to the British? An assessment has seldom been made to find out if his opposition to some of the measures of the mass movement led by Mahatma Gandhi was favourable for the country or harmed the cause of freedom itself. Did the British actually trust his alleged loyalty or even buy his so-called willingness to yield or were they forever suspicious of the dangers he posed to them till the very end? These are the litmus questions by which one must evaluate Savarkar's long continuum of petitions, and here the scales of history do tilt considerably in his favour.

His book *Six Glorious Epochs of Indian History* provides an account of Hindu resistance to invasions of India from the earliest times. It is based on historical records (many of them dubious), exaggerated accounts of foreign travellers, and the writings of colonial historians. Savarkar's own febrile and frightening imagination reworks these diverse sources into a tome remarkable for its anger and hatred.

Savarkar's account of Hindu resistance is also a history of virtues. He identified the virtues that proved detrimental to India and led to its conquest. He expounded his philosophy of morality in Chapter VIII, *Perverted Conception of Virtues*, in which he rejected the idea of absolute or unqualified virtue. "In fact virtues and vices are only relative terms," he said.

17

Pavan Kulkarni's Views on Savarkar's Petitions

Pavan Kulkarni, a freelance journalist, says about his petitions: "We all know that Savarkar was one of the biggest freedom fighters. He was arrested because English Government felt that he could help India become independent. He was kept in jail because that was in favour of English Government. He asked for forgiveness at multiple occasions, we all know that. Why did he ask for forgiveness, only he knew? May be he wanted to be out to fight through a different methodology, may be he was a coward!"

There are archived letters in UK where Savarkar's Lawyer forwards letters to the Viceroy asking for clemency where he includes the line "I have since realized that protesting against the legitimate reforms proposed by Messrs Morley and Minto was wrong, and I have regretted my actions." He also wrote more clemency letters where he clearly recognizes the Britishers as the rightful rulers.

He wrote pamphlets where he encouraged Hindus to support the British in the war and encouraged Hindus to join the war to learn about the art of war using phrases that One Day Hindus would have to defend them.

18

Trailokyanath Chakravarty's Views on Savarkar

Trailokyanath Chakravarty was an Indian independence activist and politician. He was born on 2nd August, 1889 in Mymensingh, in present day a city in Bangladesh, and died on 9th August, 1970 in Delhi, India. He was incarcerated for 30 years by the British. He was the leader of the Anushilan Samiti. He led and worked with other renowned freedom fighters and led to freedom of India. He lived for 80 years, out of which he spent 30 years in jail. Some of his years in jail were in Bangladesh after Indian independence, which was under Pakistan Government. He was first arrested for his revolutionary activities in 1908. He was one of the chief accused in the Barisal Conspiracy Case of 1913, and was sentenced by the British and transported to the Andamans as a result.

Trailokyanath has written in his autobiography that conditions in the Andamans jail were very bad. He was there along with Savarkar and others. They were tortured in all sorts of ways. Savarkar, who was older, told them to go on a hunger strike which they did. But Savarkar himself did not join it. Chakravarty told him, "How dare you not join us when you have instigated us." Savarkar was actually a hard hidden evil element who had betrayed him. So how can we make Savarkar a role model? — He added."

19

Bipan Chandra's Views on Savarkar's Portrait

Bipan Chandra, a great historian, specializing in economic and political history of modern India and an emeritus Professor of modern history at Jawaharlal Nehru University, is disappointed at the installation of Vinayak Damodar Savarkar's portrait in the Central Hall of Parliament. To his mind, Savarkar cannot be regarded as a role model. His portrait alongside Mahatma Gandhi's in the Central Hall of Parliament is a frivolous act befooling country and countrymen. He had a grievous objection to installing his portrait in the Parliament Hall, for its very sight seems to be displeasing. The act of putting up a statue or portrait in the Parliament Hall is not simply to honour a person. Portraits of great men in the Parliament Hall are supposed to be role models for citizens. In every country, including ours, young people come in busloads to be shown around Parliament. The purpose is that they should emulate a, b, c, d, etc. as their role models. He says- It is wrong to put Savarkar's portrait in Parliament Hall. Young people should not be told to emulate him as their role model.

20

Self-Glorification of a Defeated Man

One might have argued in 1924 that the promises Savarkar made about his love and loyalty to the British, about his readiness to serve the government in any capacity required and so on were a part of a tactical ploy – perhaps one inspired by Shivaji – employed to make his way out of prison so that he could continue his freedom struggle. However, history has proven him to be a man of 'honour', who stood by the promise he made to the colonial government. How then, one might wonder, did Savarkar acquire the title 'Veer'?

A book titled *Life of Barrister Savarkar* authored by Chitragupta was the first biography of Savarkar, published in 1926. Savarkar was glorified in this book for his courage and deemed a hero. And two decades after Savarkar's death, when the second edition of this book was released in 1987 by the Veer Savarkar Prakashan, the official publisher of Savarkar'swritings, Ravindra Ramdas revealed in its preface that "Chitragupta is none other than Veer Savarkar."

In this autobiography masquerading as a biography written by a different author, Savarkar assures the reader as under:

"Savarkar is a born hero; he could almost despise those who shirked duty for fear of consequences. If once he rightly or wrongly believed that a certain system of Government was iniquitous, he felt no scruples in devising means to eradicate the evil."

Without mincing words in the name of modesty or moderating the use of adjectives in the name of literary minimalism, Savarkar wrote that Savarkar "seemed to possess no few distinctive marks of character, such as an amazing presence of mind, indomitable courage, and unconquerable confidence in his capability to achieve great things". "Who," he asked about himself, "could help admiring his courage and presence of mind?"

Perhaps in polite society, we ought to quietly look the other way with an embarrassed smile when an ex-revolutionist, after breaking down in prison, indulges in self-glorification under the cover of a pen name after his release. And, indeed, no one, who did not suffer the conditions of that infamous prison on the Andaman Islands, can claim the right to castigate Savarkar for refusing to contribute to the freedom movement after he was released from jail.

But his purporting of an ideology which destabilised the freedom movement by deepening the divisions along sectarian lines, and his active rendering of support to the British government—which was determined to subdue the anti-colonial struggle—was a betrayal that must be hard to forgive, especially for a 'patriot' and a 'nationalist'.

21

Savarkar's Collaboration with the British

Savarkar was elected as the president of the Hindu Mahasabha in 1937, the year when the Indian National Congress won what we today call a landslide victory in the provincial elections, decimating both the Hindu Mahasabha and that other communal party, the Muslim League, which failed to form a government even in Muslim-majority regions. But just two years later, the Congress relinquished power in protest when, at the outbreak of the Second World War, the viceroy, Lord Linlithgow, declared India to be at war with Germany without any consultation.

"The situation, he [Savarkar] said, was that His Majesty's government must now turn to the Hindus and work with their support. Our interests were now the same and we must, therefore, work together. Our interests are so closely bound together, the essential thing is for Hinduism and Great Britain to be friends and the old antagonism was no longer necessary. The Hindu Mahasabha, he went on to say, favoured an unambiguous undertaking of Dominion status at the end of the war."

Two months later, addressing the Mahasabha's Calcutta session, Savarkar urged all universities, colleges and schools to "secure entry into military forces for youths in any and every way." When Gandhi had launched his individual *satyagraha* the following year, Savarkar, at the Mahasabha session held in December 1940 in Madura, encouraged Hindu men to enlist in various branches of British armed forces *en masse*."

"It must be noted that Japan's entry into the war has exposed us directly and immediately to the attack by Britain's enemies. Hindu Mahasabhaites must, therefore, rouse Hindus, especially in the provinces of Bengal and Assam as effectively as possible to enter the military forces of all arms without losing a single minute."

In reciprocation, the British commander-in-chief, "expressed his grateful appreciation of the lead given by Barrister Savarkar in exhorting the Hindus to join the forces of the land with a view to defend India from enemy attacks," according to Hindu Mahasabha archives perused by Shamsul Islam.

It was under these circumstances that Savarkar not only instructed those serving in the British army to 'stick to their posts', but had also been involved for years in organizing recruitment camps for the British armed which were to slaughter the cadres of INA in different parts of North-East later." In one year alone, Savarkar had boasted in Madura, one lakh Hindus were recruited into the British armed forces as a result of the Mahasabha's efforts.

Even though the British Army, with which Savarkar and the Hindu Mahasabha were collaborating, managed to defeat Bose's INA, the subsequent public trials of INA officers at the Red Fort roused in the Indian soldiers of the British armed forces a political conscience, which played a crucial role in triggering the Royal Indian Naval Munity in 1946, after which the decision was made by the British to leave India.

22

Savarkar with the Muslim League

That Savarkar and the Hindu Mahasabha actively collaborated with the British may not be difficult to comprehend, since it is widely known that the Hindutva groups regarded Muslims, and not the British, as their primary enemies. What is likely to raise more eyebrows is the collaboration of the Hindu Mahasabha with the Muslim League.

When the Congress leaders were arrested during the Quit India movement, the Hindu Mahasabha, still presided over by Savarkar, entered into a coalition with the Muslim League to run the governments in Sindh and Bengal – a move Savarkar justified as "practical politics" which calls for "advance through reasonable compromises."

After all, in spite of the deeply-held conviction by Savarkar and his party that the Muslims – whose holy land lies in a foreign country – cannot be regarded as Indian nationals, the Hindu Mahasabha nevertheless had a great deal in common with the Muslim League. Both parties made no contribution to the struggle for independence from the colonising empire and both were communal parties whose ideologies antagonised the prospects of India remaining undivided after independence.

Even after the Sindh Assembly passed a resolution in 1943 demanding that Pakistan be carved out of India as a separate state for the Muslims, the Mahasabha Ministers continued to hold their positions in the coalition government. Not entirely surprising, given that Savarkar had "a clear sixteen years before the Muslim League embraced the idea of the Hindus and the Muslims as two distinctive nations and demanded the division of India." And when India was eventually partitioned, Savarkar blamed Gandhi for allowing Pakistan to break away from India, an accusation that stoked the fires of hatred against Gandhi among many of his close devotees, including his 'lieutenant'— Nathuram Godse.

23

Was Savarkar a Traitor?

After 1937, Veer Savarkar started traveling widely, serving as the president of the Hindu Mahasabha political party. Savarkar endorsed the idea of India as a Hindu Rashtra (Hindu Nation). He had said: Hindu is the one who considers the land of Hindustan, from the Ocean to the Sindhu river as their fatherland and Holy land.

No, certainly not. He was not a traitor. He was surely a fascist supporter, communalist and a hater of non Indian based religions. All the riots, killings and lynchings happening in India to minorities are based on his ideology and beliefs.

One of the charges on Savarkar was abetment to murder of Nashik Collector, Jackson. The second was waging a conspiracy under Indian penal code 121-A against the King Emperor. Following the two trials, Savarkar, then aged 28, was convicted and sentenced to 50-years imprisonment and transported on 4 July 1911 to the infamous Cellular Jail in the Andaman.

Had he been a traitor, British Government would have treated him softly. He would have got all the limelight from British media and English press so that he would have been promoted as Indian leader and some or the other way his leadership would have been enforced on Indian public.

He was transferred from Andaman only because British government had decided to wind up the set up of cellular jail in Andaman. Till 1911, Britishers enjoyed making the freedom fighters to suffer atrocities in the confines of Andaman. After arrival of Savarkar, the inmates of jail were successful in posting the report:

1. We cannot call him a traitor. Every person has a threshold of pain. He was put in Kala Pani. Worst of the worst. When you compare jails, political prisoners of Congress were mostly given class-A jails. There they wrote great books and passed their time

by reading and learning. But that was not the fate of Savarkar.

2. The cellular jail was any prisoner's worst nightmare. Thousands perished without a trace there. No tears shed for them. They were just removed from main India to suffer the worst agony.

The only aim of Savarkar's life was to serve the country in whatever capacity. He had an absolute brilliant mind and many facets to his personality. Apart from being a revolutionary, he was a poet, a writer, a reformist and a thinker. He just decided that if he is released, he can serve the nation in many other capacities which he did. Not everyone needs to die for his country. People can also live for the country and serve her. So where is the question of being a traitor?

Really, he was not a traitor. He was a true freedom fighter as most of the other fighters. He had a deep love and respect for the country. He said that when country is in danger, one must come together and fight for the country. He was really a true patriot and brave revolutionary fighter.

But he was surely a traitor to his family. Instead of repaying their faith and efforts taken for his upbringing with great comforts available to foreign returned graduates of the time, he went holidaying to Andaman beaches for a few years leaving them back in India.

He was a shrewd politician knowing how to wiggle out of difficult situations. He was not what he made out to be. He was a good theoretician for Akhand Bharat and Hindu religion, but he only preached and never practiced. He was not an ordinary intelligent man who knew where to stop.

It is no surprise — both Mahatma Gandhi and Indira Gandhi spoke in praise of Savarkar, although it was of his pre-Hindutva revolutionary years. "I had the pleasure of meeting him in London. He is brave. He is clever. He is a patriot" — the Mahatma wrote.

Indira Gandhi's praise also came after Savarkar's death. Speaking as Prime Minister, she called him "a great figure of contemporary India" and "a byword for daring and patriotism."

24

The Other Side of the Coin

Savarkar was actually a hard hidden hero, somewhat dubious. Not only did he pledge his allegiance to the British in return for being released from prison, his propagation of Hindutva hurt the freedom movement by dividing society along sectarian lines.

Vinayak Damodar Savarkar (1883-1966) – mythologised in popular imagination as 'Veer Savarkar' – not only refrained from participating in the freedom struggle after the British released him from prison on account of his relentless pleas for mercy, but also actively collaborated with the English rulers to whom he had declared his loyalty.

At the time when Subhas Chandra Bose was raising his Indian National Army to confront the British in India, Savarkar helped the colonial government recruit lakhs of Indians into its armed forces. He further destabilised the freedom movement by pushing his Hindutva ideology, which deepened the communal divide at a time when a united front against colonial rule was needed. Post independence, Savarkar was also implicated in Mahatma Gandhi's murder.

Such is the man who was declared by Prime Minister Narendra Modi to be "the true son of Mother India and inspiration for many people", in his twitter salutation to Savarkar on his birth anniversary on May 28, 2021. In 2015, commemorating Savarkar on his 132nd birth anniversary, the Prime Minister bowed before a portrait of the Hindutva icon in remembrance of "his indomitable spirit and invaluable contribution to India's history."

A freedom fighter he definitely was, for a certain period in the first decade of the previous century, long before he had begun articulating the notion of Hindutva. Savarkar was then an atheist and a rationalist, who had started out on a revolutionary road to rid India of her colonial yoke, asserting:

"Whenever the natural process of national and political evolution is violently suppressed by the force of the wrong, the revolution must step in as a natural reaction and, therefore, ought to be welcomed as the only effective instrument to re-throne Truth and Right."

On sailing to England to study law in 1906, Savarkar founded the Free India Society to organize Indian students studying in England to fight for independence. In a famous declaration before the society, he said: "We must stop complaining about this British officer or that officer, this law or that law. There would be no end to that. Our movement must not be limited to being against any particular law, but it must be for acquiring the authority to make laws itself. In other words, we want absolute independence."

However, when the time came to pay the price for being a revolutionary under an oppressive colonial government, Savarkar found himself converted and transformed into "the staunchest advocate of loyalty to the English government", to use his own words. This was after he was arrested and sentenced to serve 50 years in the infamous Cellular Jail on the Andaman Islands after he was found guilty of supplying the pistol that a member of the Abhinav Bharat Society used to assassinate the then collector of Nasik, A.M.T. Jackson, in 1909.

His biographers believe that writing these petitions did not amount to "cowardice," as many of Savarkar's critics allege. "By writing these petitions, Savarkar was availing of his rights as a political prisoner at that time. In my opinion, the petitions do not make him less of a revolutionary or an apologist for British rule," says MrPurandare.

Savarkar was also a man of contradictions. On the one hand, he was an outspoken political voice for the Hindus. On the other, he was a rationalist, who opposed Hindu superstition, the caste system, and worship of the cow — a sacred animal for the Hindus. But after he was charged as a co-conspirator in Gandhi's killing, Savarkar became politically "untouchable".

In 1909, the Morley-Minto Reforms brought in a slew of greater opportunities for Indians to participate in councils and education. Hence, Savarkar alludes in his petition that the need to pick up the gun no longer remained, and he was happy to join mainstream politics and work with the government towards greater constitutional participation for Indians.

"I am not asking for any preferential treatment," he said, "though I believe as a political prisoner even that could have been expected in any civilized administration in the Independent nations of the world; but only for the concessions and favour that are shown even to the most depraved of convicts and habitual criminals?" It was almost an indirect mockery of British India being uncivilized.

By 1913, Savarkar and several other prisoners began hunger strikes and non-cooperation in jail to protest against this inhuman treatment. The rest of India was blissfully unaware of the tortures their compatriots faced in Kaala Pani. Hence, articles were leaked out for publication in Indian newspapers. Savarkar's clandestine attempts to start bomb manufacturing in Port Blair alarmed the authorities. Finally, in October 1913, Sir Reginald H. Craddock, home member of the Government of India, decided to visit the Cellular Jail and interview some of the political prisoners to ascertain their grievances. Savarkar and other political prisoners—Barin Ghose, Nand Gopal, Hrishikesh Kanjilal, and Sudhir Kumar Sirkar were interviewed and allowed to submit petitions. This process was a legitimate tool available for all political prisoners in British India, just like the opportunity of defending oneself in court through the agency of a lawyer was. As a barrister, Savarkar knew the law and wished to utilize all provisions under it to free himself or alleviate his situation in prison. Savarkar often advised other political prisoners too that the primary duty of a revolutionary was to free him from the British clutches so as to return to the freedom struggle and in service of the motherland.

To summarize, Savarkar started out as a hard-hearted revolutionary, abjectly renounced his principles in the Andamans, refused to join his fellow prisoners in their struggle there, stayed away from all anti-British activities after his release from prison, and, with his virulent anti-Muslim campaign, ended up helping the British in their policy of 'divide and rule'.

This is because Savarkar very explicitly stated that a change of religion implies a change of nationality. It was Savarkar, not Muhammad Ali Jinnah, who first categorized Hindus and Muslims as two nations. From the Hindutva perspective, the two nations – Hindu and Muslim – have been locked in a continuous conflict for supremacy since the 11th century.

Later in *Six Glorious Epochs*, Savarkar adopted a distinct Nietzschean tone to cry out: "O thou Hindu society! Of all the sins and weaknesses, which have brought about thy fall, the greatest and the most potent are thy virtues themselves.

25

Specific Facts about Savarkar

Savarkar began his political activities as a high school student and continued to do so at Fergusson College in Pune. In 1904, he convened a meeting of some two hundred selected members of the Mitra Mela— a revolutionary party. The name of his party was later changed to Abhinava Bharat.

He was against foreign goods and propagated the idea of Swadeshi. In 1905, he burnt all the foreign goods in a bonfire on Dussehra.

When he went to England for higher studies, he continued his revolutionary activities and set up a front organization named 'Free India Society.'

The British sentenced him, two rigorous life imprisonments of 50 years with deportation and consfication of his property. Next to him to get such a heavy punishment was Lokmanya Tilak who got four years deportation and solitary confinement. From the point of view of Britishers and their mental slave Indians, they were traitors. Same is the view today of those who take pride in dancing to the tune of the ex-bar dancer.

Savarkar was a known freedom fighter before the controversial murder trial which put him under life imprisonment in the cellular prison in Port Blair. In 1909, Vinayak Savarkar was arrested in Britain for organizing armed revolts against the British government for the newly introduced 'Morley-Minto reforms', which had called for separate electorates for Muslims to "protect them from Hindu dominance in India."

On the contrary, they say that Savarkar should never be any subject in Freedom Fight as he was never a freedom fighter. Not because he wrote mercy petitions to British but because of his immense hatred towards other religions, especially towards Muslims. He was never given the tag of "Svatantray Veer". He himself wrote a book with the Pen name "Chitragupta" in which he mentioned him as Veer. How many of you know that Savarkar was also convicted in a rape case and was punished by London Court. As a matter of fact, Savarkar himself on record accepted that he had raped a woman, his Personnal Assistant, Mr. Limaye.

But to the general opinion of our country, Savarkar was a great patriot and visionary. His daring escape at Marsailles is well. They ask anyone, who has any doubts about Savarkar's patriotic credentials to visit the Andamans and check out Savarkar's cell in the cellular jail. It stands to reason that the British would have transported Savarkar to that hell on earth and put him in a *special* cell, only if they considered him a greater threat to their Indian empire than any Congressman of the time. Even if the theory routed in some quarters that Savarkar retracted and so was released from prison is true, I wouldn't blame him. How many human beings can withstand extreme torture? Priyadarshan's 1996 film Sazaa-e-Kaala Paani documented. Similar to how Shivaji Maharaj tactfully apologized to Aurangzeb, Savarkar apologized to the British to secure his release. Savarkar knew well that had he remained imprisoned for long, he would never have been able to propogate the Hindutva doctrine and would never have been able to introduce nationalism to the country so misled by leftist leaders of the Indian National Congress.

Having read a little more about Savarkar, I can tell you and all that he had more forethoughts than many of his peers. This is evident from his speech delivered around 1952 regarding the dissolution of the Abhinava Bharat Society. There, he specified things that if put in the right context, will directly counter the allegation of being a traitor.

He supported militarization and the British administration specifically for Indians and Hindus to gain administrative and military experience. This is specifically so that an independent India wouldn't be left rudderless. This approach might not have been in go.

In fact, Vinayak Damodar Savarkar and Mohandas Karamchand Gandhi are two sides of the same coin. Savarkar pledged guilty and begged for Clemency. Gandhi pledged guilty and agreed to send Indian troops to fight for the British crown in the Second World War. No invader has ever gone out of the country with Hunger Strikes and 'ChaleJao'. The British had already made up their mind to pull out of India soon after the World War-I. But by the time, they were about to prepare their exit, the World War-II broke out and their exit delayed.

It is true that he filed multiple mercy petitions (available in public domain) and sorry notes. He promised the British government that he will work for them when he comes out. It is a known fact that Savarkar used to receive a pension of rupees sixty per month sanctioned by the British government in 1929. I wonder how he could be a British Pensioner and a freedom fighter at the same time.

About Savarkar, the true story of the Father of Hindutva, VaibhavPurandare writes: He was not a cow worshipper. "If the cow is mother to anyone at all, it's the bullock," Savarkar wrote in his Marathi journal Kirloskar. If Hindutva is to sustain itself on cow's legs, it will go crashing down at the slightest hint of a crisis." He was scornful of cow-worship, and an admirer of science. Savarkar's traits would come as a surprise.

Purandare writes: "Savarkar abhorred the idea of consuming the animal's urine and, in some cases, cow dung. Such consumption, he believed, may have actually started as a form of punishment." The cow, no doubt, was useful "but its worship made no sense. It was time to abandon the 'native practice' of 'gau-poojan' because it was nothing short of 'buddhihatya' or 'murder of the intellect'.

Though a Brahmin, Savarkar "loved his fish and disliked all his fellow Brahmins who looked at those who relish non-vegetarian food." In the mid-1950s, when India was in the grip of famine, he riled several self-styled spiritual gurus and champions of non-fish-no-meat by saying, "The country could overcome its shortage of food if Brahmins, Jains and vegetarians took to eating fish and stop judging people on the basis of what they ate."

If you find this surprising—as I did—Purandare has a lot more to shake up our preconceived notions of Savarkar. Though the author of Hindutva, he was "hardly a practicing Hindu in the religious sense. He followed no rituals and thought God, if indeed God existed, wasn't really in the habit of responding to prayer."

On one occasion, when informed of a sadhu who boasted of crawling on his stomach from Allahabad to Haridwar, Savarkar was scornful: "He sarcastically asked who had been closer to God, considering almost all religions said that God was in the heavens above—someone who was attempting to build an airplane or fly in it or someone desperate to turn himself into a maggot."

Indeed, science was more important to Savarkar than religion. He said, "Hindus were needed to place their sacred text in closets and pick up science books instead." On sex, he said: "Sexual passion was legitimate and there was nothing wrong with giving full expression to it." During his years in England, he is reported "to have been in love with an English girl, Margaret Lawrence."

Hedgewar and Savarkar—both stated unequivocally that they do not desire independence from the British connection. On the contrary, they feel that India's destiny can be worked out in association with the British. Nobody has questioned their honour or their honesty,"

He was also allowed to meet K. B. Hedgewar, a disillusioned Congressman, who, inspired by his ideology of Hindutva, intended to discuss with him a strategy for creating a Hindu Rashtra. A few months after this meeting, in September 1925, Hedgewar founded the RSS, a communal organization which, like Savarkar, remained subservient to the British.

"He's always evoked extreme reactions. From a political revolutionary he became an untouchable and now his legacy is on the ascendant," says Mr. Purandare. But it is a legacy deeply mired in controversy and contradiction.

They say that Savarkar was a third class political leader and actually true HYPOCRITE. Self proclaimed VEER and HINDU Icon uniting with Muslim league and Jinnah to keep Congress away from power. He was talking about Hindutva, but he was hyprocite. In one of the books (Six Glorious Epochs of Indian History), he has mentioned "rape as a political tool". He also criticized Shivaji and Chimaji Appa of returning Muslim women after Muslims lost war (to save the dignity of Muslim women). Savarkar was the cheapest and third grade political leader who wanted Muslim women to be raped.

26

Savarkar: Virtues or Vices

Savarkar added that the test of determining what is virtue or what is vice is to examine whether it serves the interests of society, specifically Hindu society. This is because circumstances change, societies are always in a flux. What was deemed virtuous in the past could become a vice in the present if it is detrimental to mankind, he said.

For instance, said Savarkar, the caste system with its elaborate rules of purity and pollution helped stabilize Hindu society. But some of these rules became dysfunctional, degenerating into "seven fetters" of Hindu society.

There were seven shackles, according to Savarkar, like untouchability, bans on drinking water from members of other castes, inter-caste dining, inter-caste marriage, and sea-voyage, the ban on taking back into the Hindu fold those who were forcibly converted to Islam or Christianity, and ostracism of those who defied these prohibitions.

These "seven fetters" proved advantageous to the Muslim conquerors, wrote Savarkar, because they exploited caste rules to increase their population.

The conquerors forcibly converted Hindus who had been defeated, provided them with food and water, abducted women who were either kept as concubines or wives, certain that the ban on taking them back into the Hindu fold left them with no option but to live as Muslim, the Hindutva propounder wrote. This meant the "transformation of a man into a demon, the metamorphosis of a God into a Satan."

He cites examples from the human world too. For instance, he wrote, the African "wild tribes" kill only their male enemies, but not their women, who are distributed among the victors. This is because these tribes consider it their duty to increase their numbers through the progeny of abducted women. Similarly, he wrote that a Naga tribe in

India kills women of rival tribes whom they can't capture because they believe, rightly so, that paucity of women would enhance the possibility of their enemies dwindling in number.

It is with the "shameless religious fanaticism" of Ravana that the Muslims, from the Sultan to the soldier, abducted Hindu women, even the married ladies of Hindu royal families and notables, wrote Savarkar, adding that this was to increase the population of Muslims, to demographically conquer India, so to speak.

Savarkar is venomously critical of Muslim women who, "whether Begum or beggar", never protested against the "atrocities committed by their male compatriots; on the contrary they encouraged them to do so and honoured them for it."

Savarkar, even by his own standards, takes a huge leap by claiming that Muslim women living even in Hindu kingdoms enticed Hindu girls, "locked them up in their own houses, and conveyed them to Muslims centres in Masjids and Mosques".

Savarkar is known today as the author of the 1923 work Hindutva, the seminal text for Hindu nationalists, but what he is little known for is his staunch opposition to cow worship. The cow was, for him, a highly useful animal. But its worship, he argued, made no sense because humans needed to worship something or someone who was super-human or endowed with super-human qualities, not an "out-and-out" animal inferior to humankind.

But his standout line on the subject was that "we need cow care, not worship". He particularly abhorred the then widely prevalent habit of consuming cow urine and, in some cases, even cow dung, and believed the practice may have actually started out in ancient India as a form of punishment so that a person could "expiate his sins".

And to those orthodox Hindus who thought his views were blasphemous, Savarkar had only one sardonic thing to say: your blasphemy's far, far bigger, just see how you've crammed 33 crore deities into a cow's belly.

Savarkar's readers cannot but see that he has overturned the code of ethics and freed the Hindus from the shackles that prevent them from descending into barbarism. But Savarkar doesn't seem convinced of his persuasive powers. So under a subsection titled, *But If*, he seeks to hammer in his point. He asks readers:

In *Six Glorious Epochs*, Savarkar adopted a distinct Nietzschean tone to cry out: "O thou Hindu society! Of all the sins and weaknesses, which have brought about thy fall, the greatest and most potent are thy virtues themselves."

In the mid-1930s, the editor of famous Marathi journal Bhaala posed a question to all Hindus and answered it himself. "Who is a real Hindu? One who regards the cow as his mother?"

Savarkar did not believe India had been subjugated only during the British Raj. Unlike Nehru who put forward the idea of a 'composite culture', he saw hundreds of years of Islamic rule as an era of shackles, submission, suppression and slavery. And one of his major issues with cow worship, apart from its deadening of the mind as he saw it, was that it had "ensured" many a Hindu defeat in the past. To use a bad pun which he didn't, it had engendered cow-cowardice.

He alleged that Muslim armies had often used cows as a shield during key battles against the Hindus. When Hindu forces marched on Multan, he said, the Muslims had threatened to destroy the famous Sun temple there as a warning, and when Malharrao Holkar, a Maratha chieftain, had sought to "liberate" Kashi, the Muslims had again threatened to defile all things holy to the Hindus, Savarkar said and castigated India's majority community for backtracking at such moments for fear of being responsible for the razing of temples, the humiliation of Brahmins and cow slaughter.

He said if the Hindu Rashtra, as he saw it, was ever to be hemmed in by non-Hindu forces and there was no way out of the siege to get food, cow slaughter had to be exercised as an option. The Hindus had done considerable damage to their cause, he said, by saving a few cows used as shields by the rivals, because their survival had ultimately resulted in a far greater destruction of Hindu shrines and the setting up of abattoirs all over the country.

And he had a "final word" of indictment for those non-Hindus who saw cow slaughter as a religious duty. He said: Hindus were naïve in their worship, but they weren't cruel. Those who cut down the animal as part of their dharma were not only naïve but brutal in their religious zealotry, he said, and added that they had no right to ridicule Hindus for their beliefs. In such slaughter, Savarkar saw excessive barbarism, ingratitude and an asuric (demonic) instinct. He urged such non-Hindus to give up their "cow hate" and take up "cow care."

Even if firmly situated within the Hindutva framework and calling openly for a Hindu Rashtra, this is a surprisingly complex and often apparently contradictory opinion on a subject highly sensitive in today's India. But Savarkar's view is also perhaps unique in that both the gaurakshaks and the Youth Congress's public slaughterers of a calf in Kerala might wonder what exactly to make of him.

Savarkar breathed his last on 26 February, 1966, leaving behind him a treasure of theorizations on Hindutva, Indian nationalism and such other themes that are so relevant even today to men and women fighting for a strong, united India. His theoretical writings are considered by many to have Hindu revivalist overtones, whereas many others dispute such an evaluation.